THE JOURNEY

OF

BECOMING

YOU

BY

JAMES YOUNG

ISBN 978-0-578-24150-0

Cover design by: JAMES LEE YOUNG

Printed in the United States of America

TABLE OF CONTENTS

INTRODUCTION

What do you want to do with your life? It's a simple enough question, but for most it is one that doesn't have an easy answer. The question of direction can haunt your life for some time to come, while it seems some people roll through life without an issue. For most of us there is something missing, a thought or a block in imagination that stops us from being able to live like other people. It doesn't matter if you believe we are here for a reason or that we are simply floating through space on a ticking time bomb without any explanation as to why. The truth of the matter is you want something more.

You want a reason for your life, an unequivocal change that will bring out the real you, the person you are meant to be. In this book, we will cover several topics. For you to understand them, you must be open-minded. <u>It is important that you don't take this book as a personal attack on you.</u> This is more of a guide to understanding why you might feel like things happen to you and not to others, and how to overcome them. We all live in the same world and what one man can do another man can do. It all comes down to daily choices. Each decision you make leads to the current world you live in. Understanding that these events are connected and how they are connected is crucial to making your life what you want it to be.

In the journey of finding out what is needed to heal yourself, there are many steps to take. It's not usually one big thing that has you down but several small things that need to be repaired. Sometimes you don't even know there is a problem. We will take a look at some of the most daunting issues that seem to plague us as people and the ways I was able to fix them in myself. I will go through the steps I believe will change the way you think about yourself and show that no one's opinion but your own actually matters, so long as your opinion is appropriately leading you down a better path. Join me as we go through the journey of becoming you.

UNDERSTANDING WHY YOU'RE THE PROBLEM

All throughout my twenties, I couldn't understand why people were so reluctant to help others. As I got older though I came to find the reason this was so difficult for people to help when others felt they genuinely needed it. Surprisingly, it had nothing to do with them being stingy or greedy and had more to do with the people asking for help. It came down to this, most of the time when someone asks for help they start with a story explaining why they need the help and what the help will go to. To them the request for help sounds genuine and without it they will not be able to make ends meet. They will go on to tell you that things didn't go as planned and that they are short this month on a bill. Or they don't have gas in their car.

If you're open with yourself and go back far enough in your timeline you will find the choice you made that led you to needing help in the first place.

It's not always noticeable that you have caused the issue, but trust me it is there. And almost all of them lead to you living beyond your means.

Now, I can see how this might be confusing, but stay with me here. I'm sure you're asking yourself, "How can my car breaking down be my fault?" Well, I'm sure it isn't. However, if you need the help to get it repaired, there rests the fault to which I am referring. If you have failed to set aside an emergency fund, then you will need help when the time comes that your car breaks down or you need to buy a plane ticket to get home to see a dying family member. Any time you ask for help, your ability to do things right in the future is delayed. Because now instead of saving the money for future events, you have to pay back someone before they get angry, and this cycle repeats itself indefinitely.

So how do you change this process and start to live a life that you've been waiting for? This is where things get personal. There isn't a one size fits all answer to this question. With that being said the outcome for all is roughly the same. You want to be able to support your family financially. You want to have enough money and time to take vacations. You want to live a life that is not only profitable but also enjoyable. Whatever that means to you, let's get your mind in the right place to start making the better things in life available to you.

MY TOP TEN

1)   First and most important, you must be honest with yourself. This process will not work if you are lying to yourself. If you can't get ahold of what you say to yourself or others, you will never get better. And no one likes a story teller. Show by doing not saying. People don't need to know what's going on at every turn, nor do they care. They have their own things they are dealing with.

2)   You need to know what your abilities are and where they end. Do not cross this line, or you are destined for failure. Before you do anything, make sure it is something you plan to finish. If you don't think it's going to get done, don't feel bad about it just know it is something you're not going to do and move on. There's no need to torture yourself doing things that won't get finished. It makes you hate yourself and makes others think less of you.

3)   Starting today, do your best to not ask for help from anyone for any reason. It may be difficult, and you will need to sacrifice to accomplish this. But if you're able to do so, you will see the financial benefits in your immediate future.

4)   Do not let anyone's thoughts of you sway your resolve. One of the largest reasons for failure, depression, anger, self-loathing, and many other negative emotions, is you listening to others about what they think of you or what you are doing.

5)   Don't EVER compare yourself and where you are to anyone else's life! They have different circumstances that have put them where they are. Focus on where you are and where you want to be.

6)   Don't let anyone who is not paying for the consequence of a decision sway what you should be doing. Everyone has advice but can only give you advice for things that are relevant in their world.

7)   Find people that are living the dream you would like to be living. Don't put them on a pedestal. Don't put them above you in any way. Learn from them and ask questions that pertain to your life. DON'T EVER ASK THESE PEOPLE FOR HELP. They will drop you quick. Most people who are successful in their own life are there by personal persistence. Everyone they come into contact with has asked them for some form of help. It's hard to find true friends when you're doing so well. Hanging with people that don't need anything from them is the norm. Become the norm.

8)   Never put anyone above you. To see your self-worth and get better, you must always feel at least equal to those around you. Funny thing is, when you start to feel this way, others opinion of you no longer matter. They may be smart, but don't sell yourself short. You are also smart; it may be in different ways, but that's what makes us unique, we are not the same.

9)   Don't become someone else for anyone. If you have to hide who you are to be around someone, that person is poison and has no right to be in your life.

10)   Don't be poison to someone else. If you're not there to support someone or if you are a burden in their world, you need to get control of yourself and stop being that person. Otherwise, people who do really care for you will walk away, and you will truly be alone. Be supportive, be helpful, or be gone.

This is what it boils down to about 95% of what happens to you in your life is either a direct cause of your actions or a reaction to your failure to plan. If you can get control of how you react to each situation, you will be able to outwit your troubles. Start living your life as part of the solution to your problems and not part of them.

To accomplish this, you have to make a conscious effort to think before you act. It needs to be in every decision you make. Going to the fast food place? Will that affect your ability tomorrow to put gas in your car? Buying that thousand dollar I Phone vs. a phone that works just as well for $200? Do you really need to stand in line for the next big thing? Are you spending your rent money? Experts will tell you that you should have about six months of living expenses in your account at all times. If you don't have that in your account, you shouldn't be doing anything extravagant until you do. Preplan everything. Set up what you're doing tomorrow, today and write it down. If you have a plan of attack for each day, you have a goal that sets you up for the next day. Don't put it off, do it now.

MAKING EXCUSES AND HOLDING YOURSELF ACCOUNTABLE

Truth is, you already know the answers, and you're just not applying them. You must be honest with yourself at all times. Don't allow yourself to think that there is some reason you are unable to succeed while so many others can. There is an answer for every question you could ask. You just need to find the answer, and possibly start asking the questions. This is impossible if you go through life assuming that nothing that happens to you is your fault. While there is a percentage of life that you can't control the number is far smaller than you think it is.

People tend to use excuses to cover up their own shortcomings. This is not a healthy practice because it allows you to find a reason for your bad experiences that don't point the finger back at you. This ideology will be very difficult to ever change for the better. When you use an excuse, it is usually not very believable, especially when you are telling someone that has already overcome those types of life issues. Some people will give excuses because they feel that the other person is judging them. Trust me when I tell you they will think less of you if you can't own up to your own shortcomings.

There is no reason to lie to another person. Own what you have done and accept the consequences of your action at all costs. Even if it was a bad idea that led you down a dark path, people are more willing to help you knowing that you understand what you have done wrong and have learned a lesson. It also makes you appear more believable in the eyes of someone that might be doing better than you. What you say truly matter, your word is all you truly have in this world. Keep it truthful and you will have the respect of all you come into contact with. If someone doesn't like a decision you have made, but you are ok with what you have done or the outcome of the situation, there is no reason to make an excuse or try to hide what you're doing. Here's a secret not everyone is the same and they would make a different choice than you. That's ok as long as you own your choices and expect no one else to pay for them. There will never be a reason to ever give an excuse.

If your car breaks down, and you don't have the money to fix it, someone might ask you why you don't have the money. You don't have to tell them anything at all. But if you do or you are asking for help be sure to include a truthful story and not something you think they want to hear. They might not like what they hear, but you are at ease knowing you have told the honest truth and not some bogus story. Owning up to your mistakes and shortfalls can be time consuming and a financial burden. Overcoming problems becomes easier in your future, and you will begin to accomplish things faster and failures will become less regular, as you hold yourself accountable for your actions. You will stop making bad decisions because you know that you are always watching. Worry more about disappointing yourself than others.

There might be things that you will say stand in your way. Maybe you have kids, and it's hard to make it all work when you have kids. True, but everyone knows people that have kids and are doing just fine. That's not a good excuse for why your life isn't working. If it was the fault of being a parent, then all parents would be doing poorly. You could say, I don't have the money to go to college and that's why nothing works. Well, I'm a high school drop out with no college experience, yet I'm owner or part owner in several businesses, so that's not it. You could say, "I was in the hospital, I lost my job, got kicked out of my house, car broke down" and many other reasons why your life isn't working, and I can show you someone in the same situation that is making life work just fine.

There is no easy answer, but to ever get to an answer at all, you need to be living in the real world. You need to understand that the relationship between your actions (or lack of action) and what you tell yourself when it comes to solving the problem have a direct effect on your future and its outcome. If you can't be honest about your own life, you never will be able to effectively make any positive changes that will benefit your future. Don't sit on the sidelines of your life and watch it move out of your control.

Here is a test I would like you to perform the next time something happens to you that appears to be out of the blue. I want you to look back into your past to find what steps you may have missed or what moment you could have done differently to change the outcome you are facing at that moment. If you can find what went wrong, you will be able to correct it in the future. Don't assume bad things are happening for no reason. Bad things almost never happen for no reason. Truly look at the steps you took and find the one you overlooked or missed entirely. Then correct it to better advance in your future.

KNOWING YOURSELF

This is such an important step in the evolution of becoming a better you that I talk about it in almost every chapter. But what does it mean? Does anyone ever truly know who they are? How do you go about finding that person if you have no idea what you want to do with your life or don't know who you want to become? I'm here to tell you that even if you don't know what you want to do with your life, you can still know who you are. It all comes down to having principles to live by, knowing what you will accept in life and what you will not. You also must know the answers of who you are before you go into any commitment.

The problem with most people is that they think either too highly of themselves or not highly enough. For instance, if you've ever started a project that didn't get finished, you might think to yourself, "Why did I start that"? I knew I wasn't going to finish it." Or you might look at something and think, "I can do that" but either someone or your own mind told you otherwise, so you never started that task. The truth is you never know if you never try. The point is to get to a spot in your own world that lets you know truly if it is something above your abilities or not. Only time and effort can give you a good perspective on that. It's not something I can answer for you. My goal is to make you aware that this can be a problem if it goes unchecked. You either will start things you don't finish or go nowhere because you never start at all. Both of these lead to you feeling poorly about yourself.

I'm telling you to get out and try, but with an open mind, you need to be honest about your abilities otherwise you will fail every time. The importance is that you try every day. Even more important is that you try the correct tasks every day, ones you know you can do. When trying new things, there always will be a learning curve, but only you can decide if it's something you should have gone for beforehand or not. For instance, let's say you'd like to build a playhouse for your kids. So you go out and buy all of the materials and start on the playhouse. The kids are excited, and you're happy with the idea of them being excited.

After a few days, you have a wall up but forgot to buy the right amount of screws. Then you lose interest and decide it's not worth finishing. You overlooked the expense of all the materials anyway and move on to something else. The kids are sad and you feel like you have failed them because you didn't get it finished. Most things in life are like this playhouse. It's not something you even had to start, but now that you have it's a burden and a touchy subject to talk about. If you start something, you should always make sure the task gets finished. To avoid these types of issues in the future some planning needs to be taken into effect. Is it something you wanted to do in the first place? If not, you should be more careful about the projects that get started. Do you have the money, time, stamina to finish this project? This is where knowing yourself and your abilities will come into play. No one said you had to build a playhouse but now that you've started just be sure it is something that you will finish. And don't feel bad if it's something people want you to do but you can't or don't want to do. It's better to let someone know that you wouldn't finish that task if asked instead of starting something and not finishing it. They may be mad if you don't want to do it that's their problem. But if you take on a task and don't finish it they will have a legitimate reason to be mad.

Knowing yourself will go a long way in the grand scheme of things. In fact everything you do is in direct relation to it. Being able to effectively calculate the outcome of a decision is what makes your life better or worse. Take the gamble out of your life by creating direct yes or no answers to all that you do. Then stand behind your decisions. You always should expect more from yourself, just be sure it's for you before you take it on. This can be applied in everything, including the job you take, the person you live with, the vehicles you drive, and more. It will determine the people you are associated with as well. You don't want to be known as the person that's full of shit. So be sure to make effective choices and tell the truth about yourself and your abilities.

DEALING WITH NEGATIVE PEOPLE

This is a hard subject to deal with considering that the most negative people in your life tend to be a family member or a spouse. More often than anyone would like to admit, family is usually the first to take the rug out from under your feet. Their aggressive words are usually disguised as advice, and they seem to know what's best for you while stepping over their own problems. These types of people usually don't have any real achievements of their own, yet somehow they are going to help your problems with their aggressive attitude toward your opinions of where your life should go. Sometimes, they don't even know they are doing it. Subconsciously, they don't want you to succeed because they fear that if you do you may forget about them. By making you feel as small as possible, what they are doing is saving themselves from feeling inadequate. This is a fight or flight response to the realization that they might not be as good as you.

This is a true negative attack on who you are, and shouldn't be taken lightly. If you're unable to make them aware of your plans without them coming undone, maybe time to consider dropping this person from your life. There is a difference between giving advice and treating people badly because you disagree with them. Make sure you know the difference. If at any time someone makes you feel badly about your ideas, you need to be very clear with them that you will not be tolerating that type of behavior if they want to continue to be around you. There is never a reason to raise your voice however; this will only set that person off further. Intelligent conversation will never be reached again. If a common ground on the topic cannot be reached move on to another conversation. They have made it clear they don't have any advice to offer you down the path you are on.

Concerning a spouse, you need to be more tactful. What the person you have decided to share your life with is saying is relevant. They may not be right, or at least your opinion of right. That being said, they do have more of a voice in your endeavors than, say, your brother would. Their aggression is also a fight or flight response but not one fueled by fear of your leaving but more of fear of the unknown or the reality that failure is possible. You have set up a life with this person, changing something can cause quite a fear for someone that is comfortable with their current life. There are some instances that may call for a separation, but that is not something I would be able to answer for you. If you're unable to work out your differences, you shouldn't be with that person in the first place.

This does take a bit of self-reflection, though; you can't just dismiss every person who disagrees with you. You first need to see where they are coming from. Are you the type of person who has said things in the past that didn't come true? Have you created past events that you have to make up for? If so, you may need to prove yourself a few times before people will once again trust you at your word. Just make sure that what they have to say is truly invalid and not them reflecting your own misguided past endeavors against you. This is a question only you can answer, but be true to yourself and to all those who call you family.

TAKING CONSTRUCTIVE CRITICISM

While there are many people who will belittle you for the way you think, taking constructive criticism is necessary. You can't just believe you are the smartest person you know and stop learning. There is always something new to learn and talking to the right people will always be beneficial in your future endeavors. Whether you have an interest in starting a business or just finding out how to effectively save a few bucks, talking to the right people is crucial.

Let's say you want to start a business in dog grooming, but you know nothing about it. Do you give up or do you seek out those who might know the answers to any questions you might have? Same if someone approaches you with what they believe to be important information. You might just learn something, so long as you're willing to listen. There are some people out there that genuinely want to see you succeed. Turning that person away might be the difference in success or failure.

This applies to any move that you can make in life. Thinking you got it all figured out is exactly the moment life puts something in your way that you weren't prepared for. Take the time to talk with people, especially those living a life style you are interested in living. Advice is easy to hear when it is in on par with your own thinking. A wise person will take advice from someone who knows when it counters your own way of thought. Even if this advice is not what you want to hear, the lesson you learn could be invaluable. You might just get ahead of the game when taking others' learned lessons into account.

Not only should you be open to criticism, you should seek it out. You might not believe this if I told you, but my spelling is terrible and my grammar is worse. The only reason this book exists in a form you can understand is because I was able to take criticism from those who know and then applied their understanding to my own methods. Being open will get you further than any place you thought possible. It will allow the growth needed for you to ever go beyond just existing in this world.

My dad was one of the worst people to talk to when I was growing up. It seemed that no matter what I did, it wasn't up to his standards. No matter what I tried to do I couldn't get his approval. I was always telling him my ideas of the future, and all I got from him in return was reasons why I wouldn't be able to make it work. But instead of seeing things from his view, I went dark, and decided that I was no longer going to tell him my ideas and stopped sharing my future with him. But guess what happened? Nothing, absolutely nothing in my life changed. He was right, I wasn't able to do the things I told him I was going to do. Not because I felt bad about myself but rather I didn't apply the knowledge my father was trying to give to me. Feeling bad about myself came later when I found out what I always knew, I wasn't going to do it anyway and I shouldn't have attempted that certain task in the first place.

My father passed away at the age of 56 On August 14, 2018. It was only after he was gone did I wish his wisdom to once again be in my life. I didn't take into account the actions I was doing to make my father feel the way he did about my abilities. When I was younger, I said much and accomplished little. I can see now that maybe he knew me better then I knew myself at that time in my life. I only wish he could have found a better way to say it. Or maybe, I could have found a better way to listen. Either way, what I am left with now is trying to remember, through my jaded wall of anger, what it was he was trying to tell me. I don't regret the relationship my father and I had. I do however find it sad that I will never be able to tell him I will be ok and that my life worked out.

I guess what I'm trying to say to you is, be open to the advice you are receiving. It really could be in your benefit. You're dismissing it as aggressive rhetoric and cutting someone out of your life without understanding your life first.

DEALING WITH LOSS

The loss of something can become so devastating that you fail to function at a normal rate for some time. No matter what people say, grieve for as long as you need. You will find that making sure you have given yourself the ample amount of time to deal with loss will make you stronger in the long run. Loss doesn't necessarily mean someone has died. There are many types of loss. Losing your job, losing your spouse, a car was repossessed, you have failed at a task you felt strongly about. Whatever it may be, just make sure you have recovered from the loss before attempting to be normal again. Remember, people that haven't been through a similar circumstance won't understand. So take what they say with a grain of sand. But be there for someone else if you see them struggle with loss. It is a terrible thing to go through alone.

Be sure to give yourself time. The last thing you need is to be getting back out there only to repeat the same mistakes again. As you go through life, doing something over and over and failing at it can be one of the worst things for morale. If you haven't learned anything from your past, the future will be more difficult to deal with physically and mentally. You have to understand what went wrong and how you will move past it next time. This is only achieved when you are grieving and doing some self-reflecting. When you have the answers to go out and try again, you will come at it from different angles or perspectives that give you the edge you need to make sure it won't happen again.

You also need to be sure the thing in which you are grieving for is worth the time in the first place. If you find that the pain is too great or the thing isn't worth the grieving, then be sure that when you're done grieving and you have some answers, that you don't fall back into tasks, efforts, poor decision making, or relationships that won't be worth the time it takes to get over them. You are in a constant battle of the easy way and the right way. Don't let yourself fall into the "easy way" state of mind. I promise the first mile is easy; getting to the finish line will be impossible. Do things right the first time and you won't end up repeating mistakes you've already made along the way.

LETTING GO OF STUFF

Let go of the things in your life that hold you down. We've already talked about negative people in your life. But those aren't the only things weighing you down on a daily basis. An example of another thing would be your lifestyle. Yes, the way you live could inadvertently be causing you hardships you didn't even know are hardships. That car payment, insurance, the unlimited streaming TV, radio, cable, Internet, phone, subscriptions you pay for. Don't look now, but we are over $1000 a month in crap that didn't need to be, and how do you reward yourself? By buying things you don't need to make up for the crappy job you have and the boring life you lead. This in turn keeps you at that crappy job you have and prevents you from doing anything other than the boring things you're doing right now.

That's not even scratching the surface of things you need to let go of. What about all that stuff in your garage that you haven't looked at since you were like 12? Or those projects in the basement that you will someday get to that sit there year after year? Good news is the cause is the cure here. Believe it or not, getting rid of things is like a weight being lifted off your shoulders. With every piece of crap you throw away or every subscription you quit paying for, the load of responsibility becomes lighter. The house seems bigger, the place smells better. The family can move around without knocking things off of the shelf. Everyone in the household will benefit from this action.

It's a win-win for all involved, you are happier and in turn the spouse is happier, the kids aren't sure what's gotten into you. All the sudden, you have the money to go out and do things. I promise, you won't even miss the TV. Getting rid of stuff isn't for everyone just be sure the things you keep around are contributing a positive in your life and not a negative. But if you sit down and really go through your stuff you will probably find that most of it means absolutely nothing to you and you're not sure why you've kept it around so long in the first place. If you can get your head around what is helping you and what is hindering you. Your life will continue to move in a positive and constant direction forward.

CREATING PATTERNS OF SUCCESS

There have been several studies on how the brain functions. In short, it creates pathways directly linked to the things you do every day. Going from learning a thing to knowing it so well that sometimes you don't even know you're doing it. You have put yourself on autopilot without even knowing it was a thing. Those of you that use an alarm clock to wake up in the mornings, how often do you wake up just before the clock goes off? Or those of you that as soon as you wake up you go directly to your phone to see what's happening today.

What happens when the alarm doesn't go off or your phone is not where you though it was? Your body goes into a panic, the severity of which differs from person to person, but your brain has in fact created a pathway that is now a habit. And now your body tells you that any straying from that habit is wrong and not the way things are done. How often have you forgot to kiss your spouse goodbye and had to come back into the house to do so before you left? Both of you noticed something was different.

Creating patterns is our brains way of making your life as efficient as possible. They work exactly as programmed, but most people don't realize they are the programmer. You tell your brain each day what to save and what to get rid of. This is why leaving can be so hard for some. To go from being in a bad relationship to being single, is a part of your fight or flight mechanism. The habit you created being in that bad relationship now screams at you that if you leave nothing will ever be right again. Even seeing friends once a year becomes habit, like clockwork you think about the same person around the same time of year, every year without even knowing you did it. Habits form in everything we do. Being aware of them is what will give you the ability to change them.

Some people have a habit of leaving, no matter what is going on in the outside world. Their brain has told them their time is up, and they leave, or maybe you're the person that thinks you are in a hurry even when you're not. Being stuck in one place is not enjoyable because your brain is telling you that you have something to do all the time, even when there is nothing else to do.

So how do you change the patterns so you can have something else? Well it sounds cliché, but to get something you've never had you will have to do something you've never done. And that's a fact, Jack. Before you can even think of your next step, you will have to convince yourself that it is the right one. It will be an argument with yourself and probably anyone you share your life with because they have the same problem of habit. Being logical in thought and being logical in execution are totally different. An idea can be logical when you're thinking about it, but as soon as you try to implement the change into your life, the brain hits the reverse switch and starts the countdown to the panic mode of what ifs and negative thought.

Usually if your brain is telling you something is a bad idea but in logic you know it's a good idea, you should go for it, because the regret of not knowing what you're capable of is worse than a possibility of failure. To quote Suzy Kassam "Fear has killed more dreams than failure ever could". So let's start small so your brain doesn't tell your heart to go into arrest mode. You can start off with small changes and work your way up to the larger ones. Say you want to get to a point where you can save money with ease, but the brain tells you that you need that money to get by.

Ok let's start with a smaller daily task, like making sure to put the socks in the hamper instead of the floor every day until it becomes so ingrained you forget it was a task to begin with. After that, start putting the dishes you use in the dishwasher instead of in the sink. Eventually that task will become second nature.

If you do enough of these changes, the brain will accept them easier and without as much of a fight. For one, you know firsthand that you can in fact make the necessary changes. Your brain knows it can trust you because the changes you made were successful. Probably the most important thing to happen is changing something on a regular basis until it becomes a habit. Don't worry if it doesn't happen overnight; nothing worth doing happened overnight. It is a battle, but if you play the long game you will win and create the habits of success. It is as simple as doing a task over and over until it becomes habit. That is roughly about 20 times by the way, so count them down when you start.

CREATING A DIET FOR MENTAL HEALTH

Food goes a long way in achieving mental health. Everything from creating energy to having good teeth comes into play when you talk about what you are consuming. Now I'm not here to tell you what you should be eating. That is something only you and your physician can come up with. But I will tell you if you get your food from a window or you can cook in less than 3 minutes in a microwave at home, it's probably not good for you and those types of food should be eaten in moderation.

Food is amazing if you think about it, it can cure things like sleep deprivation, depression, obesity, diabetes, and many other forms of ailments that plague the human population. Be careful, though; food is also the leading cause of the same diseases mentioned above. I'm not a fan of following a diet, but at some point in your life you have to realize the effect the food you are eating is having on you. I will admit I'm an avid "from a window" food kind of guy. But in recent years I've noticed that I'm not the same person I used to be. Sure I can chalk it up to just getting older and call it a day. But there's no way I'm living into my sixties feeling the way I do at 36, something needs to change.

Part of effectively changing is knowing yourself and what you are capable of. I know I will never be the fruits and veggies only kind of person. But is there room to improve? There sure is; it is a matter of taking the time to make the effective changes one would want to see become a reality. Just like anything else, change won't happen overnight but without an attempt for it, the change won't happen at all.

There is a certain social aspect that comes with eating; food is often a shared event. Even at work, food is consumed, usually in a group setting. So just going to the healthy side isn't going to work in my opinion. Being healthy, I believe, is a good balance of nutritious foods and foods you actually enjoy eating. Does this mean we get pizza? Sure, but don't eat the whole damn thing! And don't eat it every day. I have found what works best for me isn't so much of what I eat but how much of it I actually eat.

Being tired is something that comes with over eating bad foods. So is low energy and depression. Ever notice how sick you feel after going out to a buffet and getting your money's worth of whatever they have there but eating the same amount of greens or salads doesn't make you feel the same way? Well, clean foods don't tend to come with the terrible side effects like, food coma.

Trying to accomplish anything after too much food is hard to do. Now think about it, if you eat bad food every day, how long before you don't want to do anything ever? You go to work, have a huge lunch, come home and sit on the couch. What kind of positive life changes do you ever plan to accomplish when you literally fall asleep after every meal?

Or even worse, you're like me where you don't eat all day, come home and have a large dinner just before bed. This also has bad side effects, as you starve yourself all day then just before hibernation, you eat as much as you can, effectively telling your brain to go into storage mode. If so, you probably got a belly like mine. The one where you're still a size 34 but the belly sticks out so far you can't tell if you've properly buckled your belt.

Fasting all day isn't good either, as giving yourself no energy during the day also makes it excessively hard to create appropriate change in your life for the better. Both roads lead to you doing nothing and only thinking of change. So let's go ahead and start eating like we should and make the changes that need to happen in our lives that need to be there. There are several diets out there; try a few and stick to what seems to work best for you. Create the change you want to see, and start living the life you believe you deserve.

THANK YOU

I want to personally thank you for sticking around this long to read my book and hope that you find as much fulfillment in reading it as I have found in writing it. I know that there are parts of this book that point the finger at you, but I also know that pointing the finger at yourself first will give you the best results in creating a solution to the issues you may be facing. I know that there is an answer for everyone that seeks one, and if you are searching for a better life, my friend, you will find it. Please watch for the follow-ups to this three part book series. The following books will continue the lessons I have learned in my life that I want to share with you, including a financial guide and a relationship guide yet to come.

I hope to see your faces at events in the future. I hope, too, that my books can give you clarity on many problems that seem to plague our lives. I wish you all the best in your endeavors.

-THANK YOU-

James

www.ingramcontent.com/pod-product-compliance
Lightning Source LLC
LaVergne TN
LVHW051207080426
835508LV00021B/2855